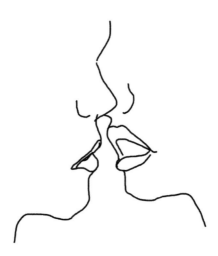

love

make love

calm as settling dust
I break easy at the knees
sheets are clinging
and we are bathing in a silent hunger
as the night draws in
we dissolve into dancing fire
a sweat drenching heat
a burning somewhere deeper
unaware of the quiet rain
or the expired sun
we run home like
skipping stones

[on sundays]

I fell for her
I fell for her hard
and when she used to squint at the sky
I'd
spend my time
marveling the many lashes
that acted
like curtains for her fucking brilliant
storm coloured eyes

I'm not sure where she took me
it was hot,
I remember
her rays, like the sun's, penetrated
my heart
and when the days seemed to roll by
I'd
spend my last dime to make them stop
to keep her face in my mind
to forget how it hurt
and her hands tucked
in the creases
of my
button down
shirt

[at church]
[on sundays]

There were days, I remember,
when I couldn't forget
the way her hair blew in the midnight wind

dawn. dusk.

there was a time when I did not know moonlight
tranquility:

the space between awake and asleep for longing
glances, soft touches and desperate lips when
eyelashes kiss tenderly; a million unused wishes
when slowly, deep breathing recedes as the room is
bathed in a comforting darkness the moon creeps
past the expansive reach of the window as hands
reach out to hold onto each other a practiced
searching that proves you are not alone

there was a time when I did not know sunrise
dreaming:

the space between asleep and awake for tired
smiles, gentle back-baring masterpieces and
entangled stretches when cheeks are stamped with
pillow creases; a thousand ornate folds when
slowly, eyes adjust to morning light as the birds
sweep past singing the sky is a promising grey, the
kind that gives you hope (like your eyes)as the sun
stays tucked behind a practiced hiding that proves
we are in the northern hemisphere

jack.

honey — sweet
sea cliffs and homemade contraptions
improvised flying

fall asleep, fingertips on screen
awaiting vibrations
cheek kisses accompany
the beating of drums
red

what is ninety-six times sixty?
too long.

grey with a tint of blue,
we shift from head in lap
to chin on chest

if I lean my forehead
against your forehead
can I see all of your dreams?

kendrick kisses and canines
mud-laden boots and half crescent smiles
humble hums and calloused hands
quilted sand dunes and no to sardine sandwiches

I'll send my promises to grace you mind
before you drift to sleep
so you feel safe among the sheets

the crater that inhabits your cheek
reminds me of the moon
and when her lunar face greets the night sky
my mind shifts to you

mud-slides and restless wind
fingertips inching closer and closer
sincere and staring through screens
into the endless oceans of computing power—
this is us

imperfection

Let me paint you and frame you in rococo
bordered by gold
you deserve to be worshiped by their eyes

Let me paint you the satsuma colour
that the sky turns during sunset
resist not, you are lovely this way

Let me paint you with nothing on
beautiful as the day you were born
your focus alleviated upwards towards the heavens

Let me paint you as you would be on the ceiling of
the Sistine Chapel
you belong there among the cherubs
you have not been displaced

Let me paint you in a humid flurry
ochres and maroons
an engraving of these words along the frame:

spare me not, from your judging gaze
for I am perfect in my imperfectness

lucky

give me honey and bamboo shoots
I will show you how I love you so

be gentle with my edges
they curl into themselves when not taken care of

don't buy me diamonds
fresh strawberries are the key to my heart

find a silence to offer me a smile
and I will yell from the barren roof top
how lucky I am to know you

suede kisses

getting to know her was like trying out a new sofa
her skin, softened suede
worn with time, but better off for it
her eyes, grandfather clocks
keeping count, quite aware, very wise

she'd spend days with her head in a book
drinking up stories, absorbing new knowledge
her voice, soft rain in the middle of July
I sat listening and cherishing each word
as it left her lips

her laugh rung like church bells on Sunday
playing a tune that I could never forget
a tune my heart would play percussion for

she never put herself first
a sun, she let all her warmth flood out of her
to help those who needed beautiful chandeliers
of light to admire

of course she cried too
like everyone does, but never did a tear escape
her weary eyes without prudence
that soul of hers, like lockets passed on through

generations
had lived many lives before and had known many
stories too

a fiery girl, burning bright
I was lucky to have soaked in her rays
and to have been ignited by her sparks
bathed in her rivers and memorised her canyons
and peaks
oh, my masterpiece

maybe

she waits. she anticipates.

the door is opening, he's smiling a smile
that fell off his face last November.
he's holding some daisies, he remembered,
maybe.
feet shift, wind wakes, and a scent from lifetimes
before turns her hollowed heart into a cave full of
crystals;
easily broken.
coffee or green tea sits between them, she's not
sure which one he likes anymore.
strawberry daiquiri still?
they talk, reminisce, hold hands, and the rain starts
to fall;
she can hear the sound. she can hear the sound; the
sound of the radiator humming to the saddest
tune. her heart's beating too.
the coffee is cold.

nomad

my mother told me to find rhythm
smooth like sandstone, smooth like
have you ever felt her skin?
plain and planed, I roam her grounds
and it grounds me

if I were to close my eyes
find a new home somewhere between Buffalo, NY
and her hips
I'd be happy

you can tell when her mind drifts to him,
pretend not to notice the marks he has left on her
body
pretend not to mind when he
steals away

she stole it, an organ
it has no home
migrating through promises
led on by misinterpreted silences
she silences my mind by telling me she loves me
and I mind this time, because I know the love she
has
in mind is not the kind
my organs long for

my mother taught me to dress
well in silk and lace, lace like
have you ever caught a glimpse of her long legs
beneath layers of petticoats?
wounded and wound, I admire her ruins
and it ruins me

the worst part is:
she has no intention to
prevent the intention of my wounds, I
travel her looking for a home and I have yet to find
one

software

If I could love with every fibre in my body
I would
but I know it would cause more damage than
you're prepared for
committing to your dreams isn't the same as
committing to an alive human being
the back and forth is constant
and its not the "how are you doing" 's that matter
its the bath of uncertainty and mistrust
that they drown themselves in
as hard as we try to keep our tones from
straying
your slight inflictions and the rhythm of your
speech is not a song
my heart can find a beat to
each slip up indicates the hopefulness
we had installed in this software that is
anything but cashmere and far from velvet
but I knew the system would fail
too many distractions under your belt that
you aren't willing to get rid of
at least next time
I'll invest in someone with a greater
hard disk capacity

enough.

some time ago
I would have laughed at the thought of
finding love
now I gaze upon it with fondness
a nostalgic confusion
a pre-existing notion of
who is meant to be loved by whom and
why did I think I was not enough?

remains.

this is how I awaken
having forgotten that being in your arms is warm
enough to thaw my heart out
are we there yet?

this is how I fall into unconsciousness
knowing that you are alone and floating space
wide
gone from this stratosphere
are you high yet?

this is what is left:
a forest green sock (you must have the other one),
a note scrawled illegibly across a sticky note— still
stuck to the fridge, a hat that says 'I'm not your
bitch', a worn copy of Catcher in the Rye without
its cover and with a permanent indent in the spine
that leads to page 108

this is how I feel
more upset at the lack of being held than
your freckled arms holding me
can you care yet?

this is what I think
you were a whirlwind of unfortunate that just
happened

to be good at enveloping for comfort but until the
point of choking
have you grown yet?

I hope you've grown.

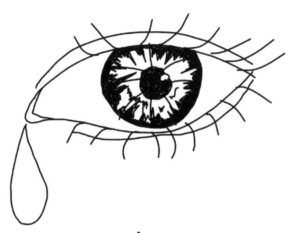

grieve

tom.

a bright light opens the door
stays by the door
holds it open for everyone who passes through

my first memory of you

you were a blessing
sent by no one but your own heart's keeper
keeping the beat

you were a star
the brightest ones are actually planets you know?
you were a planet
and we were your moons
effected by your gravitational pull
falling into orbit

you were a tree
constantly growing, always nurturing
giving those in danger a safe place to rest
beneath your branches

you were the waves
beating against the eastern shores of Scotland
sure, steady, humble yet confident

only impassioned in the wake
of a storm worth fighting for

you were the rays of sunlight
decorating the walls in the afternoon
bright, golden, illuminating
helping us see the beauty
before our eyes

you were the soft melody
floating on the breeze
enveloping the saddest individuals
in an uplifting embrace

you were baseball caps
turned backwards
and mismatched socks
in worn out shoes

you were wide toothy smiles
and wildly waving hands

you were love unconfined

now you live on in the chest of a woman
who couldn't breath
no doubt filling her heart

with the same love you possessed
because that love was far reaching
and far from isolated in your mind

that love flowed far beyond your neural pathways
though you might have tried to convince me
otherwise
saying 'feelings are chemical reactions in the brain'
well then explain the love
that I heard in your every breath
that love coursed through your veins
like molten lava

so somewhere a woman is
breathing your love into the atmosphere
and with every exhalation
making it a warmer place

I'm looking out across the water and the stars look
a little less bright tonight
except for one…
the brightest ones are planets you know?

soldier on

your portrait: stained with confusion
a fitted form of communication
lingers
ink on palm
mouth, red, from catapulting insults
proof of tenacity
she says
and further on
a near-by call to arms

souls that part

Souls that part
End up finding each other again.
Maybe not in a wide-toothy smile,
But in the way the stars flicker
like a bulb nearing the end
Of its expectancy.
Maybe not in porcelain skin
Dotted with freckles and scars,
But in the way the wind hums
Through the trees and the leaves.
Maybe not in the curvature and depressions
In the shape of her body,
But in the way the sky seems to extend forever
And in the way that days may seem endless.

words

the words, new, unfolding at the mouth
some of him trapped in his side
steeped in a night's mist
his exoskeleton bathing in cynicism

broken for chosen reasons
the oil slick of his hair, tendrils dipped in the right
side of his face
shines defiantly among the black and the bullshit

walking out of the world, he holds on tightly
with his left hand, concealed
the right swings daringly by his side

ready for decease
he lets go
go
gone

despite

quiet mournings
deceased; you wake
a blanket of lilies
a soft organ melody
tinted blue, the world keeps turning
despite

somber afterlives
undead; you awake
a haze that covers
a hum that's constant
tinted red, the world keeps turning
despite

silent evenings
tired; you'll sleep
an overwhelming nothingness
a pin drop silence
tinted green, the world keeps turning
despite

reprise

please
reprise your role.
though you now reside far beyond
where the moon-raker grazes the sky
I will crochet a hammock to catch you as you fall
do you hear me?
your reticence unnerves me
stars like stratified light bulbs
flicker
but which one are you?

how to say goodbye

Auf wiedersehen

Hold on tight until palms sweat
and muscles ache
I will not let you go lightly
or softly, I am sorry

Au revoir

The eyes that saw my first step,
the hands that held me close,
the lips that whispered guidance
the hearts that warmed my soul

Adiós

It will not be graceful
I do not know life without you
open windows and Belgian chocolate bear your
names
every possession, a link to you

Tchau

I hope it goes something like
grey hair and frail bones,
peaceful and while dreaming,
forty years from now or never

survive

red yellow black blue

I wore you like a bruise.

Indigo and mustard, you coloured me over time.

A patch of honour, a symbol of survival so often mistaken for

a love bite.

Though long gone, your aura remains;

This time a crimson red and midnight blue.

This time a mark to remember you by as the hurt slowly fades and I still feel used.

rose garden

you are a rose garden
blooming uninhibited
do not let him tread upon your bed
do not let him rip your petals off the stem
do not let him paint you any colour but red

you are a rose garden
growing footloose
do not let him fence you in
do not let him find a way to uproot you
do not let him blame you for his sins

learn to puncture.
no more getting by, by getting by.
your thorns are your best friend.

inner voice

criticism, ripe in her mouth
she has slapped a bulletin board on your face
it reads: punish.
arid sounding voices tune into the channel
hardly a delay
before they are wide-eyed and barking at you.
pessimistic chants swoop in
and then they've set off the smoke alarm.
a deafening signal caressing your eardrums
and all you want is for it to cease
but she will race you to the finish line
and wager a deal that means she gets to stay.

how to find your God

Before you begin,
clear out the room; make space.
Do not begin to imagine that there are any
boundaries.
Everything is free game.

If you start off broken, you're right (fine)
the ambiguity will trample on your spirits before
you manage to
pray at night, so
enjoy your conviction.

Go hiking slightly north of 'how was the earth
created?' and bayonet
the teeming soil with your flag of doubt;
this expedition has only just begun.

Watch the roots of trees, once vigorous, realise
their way up the mast
just as they begin to tear it down, they decay; a
heap of church bells rusting.
Doubt stands strong.

Do not try to dig for beings, pre-existing
I'm afraid, you won't find the key to open the
chest.

Innards spill from the gaps in the hinges and your
hands are bloodied with the tearing apart of
someone else's God.

Scale rocky faces; clinging, with calloused palms,
onto jagged edges

pray you find a cave of answers half way up the
cliff side

but you settle when it becomes clear just how hazy
this journey has become.

after a storm

The storm will pass, she reminds herself
air made thick by steam
suffocates her;
words cannot find an escape
but
Beethoven's sonata 7
softens the air
for a while.

her body is cold though a constant cloak
of hot water rains down
upon it
searing damages of past storms
deeper and deeper;
supple skin littered with
scars that form
beautiful constellations
tragic situations

all hot flaming stars that burnt out
years ago
but have a way of reminding.

salty tears mix with
droplets on glass
that glow

triumphantly golden.
hot water disappears
chilling her body until
her physical numbness
mirrors her emotional one.

no one's there

Something moves and I stare out the window
longing for something
crisp fall mornings would envy

the emptiness is palpable
yet comfortable;
feeling lonely and being alone
separate themselves like
oil and vinegar
and stillness seems alright

its been a while
since the sound of something
has made me smile
its just been quiet, I suppose;

the door bell is ringing
I don't move, but it chimes again
I'm not sure how long it takes me
to get there,
but when I answer the door
no one's there

and it's just fine
because I didn't expect there would
be anyone;

"penny for your thoughts"

his voice brings back memories
in an
overwhelming
avalanche

bridges

mind the bridges
my dear
mind the bridges you've burnt
mind the ashes
my dear
and the pages you've turned

deep

tinted green by the apocalyptic shadows,
this Tuesday feels like an afterthought.

reaching for my purse, I accidentally grab hold of a
memory;

a memory buried so deep, I thought it had died,
but by
keeping the way the ink marked the paper, I kept it
alive.

'four fifty miss' and I drop the memory;

pulled out of my reverie, I pay for my coffee and
leave.

the unknown

an ode to quivering fibres
to bones aching with nervousness
to muscles that impatiently tremor
what awaits us?
the melody finds itself as it writes itself
upon the pages we find hard to turn

Dear microwave,

You should know that I haven't slept at all.

My head is very much reminding me of all the atrocities of last night.

I didn't want to leave.

I was planning on ordering kung pao chicken and burying myself in a sea of sheets.

I guess it was fate when I slipped my frail body into a dress that I regret buying and will probably burn, now that it is soaked in

fright and unconsciousness.

All we can ever do is cross our fingers, right?

Hope with all our might that it's not our day to be torn from the ability to defend ourselves.

So, I tell myself that there is nothing I could've done and it helps to realise that the sacred temple which is my body was destroyed, not because of something I deserved but because society has not shown disdain for this kind of terrorism.

I repeat: "It is not my fault" to the rhythm of your incessant beeping, but please dear microwave, stop.

I have to be at work in an hour and I have a goddamn hangover.

emptiness

the first kind is a hallow feeling gnawing at your
bones;
digging the marrow out
letting it wither away
structures revolting

the second kind is a sickening pain clawing its way
into your chest cavity;
attaching to the ribs
letting them bow under its pressure
spaces inhabited by cancerous entities

the third kind is a numbness spreading from digits
to limbs;
turning muscle to ice
letting it crack and splinter
feeling abandoned

lost your light

The light creeps in through the
closed blinds
leaving blue and yellow stains on the
wall
the books that I fell asleep reading
last night
lay scattered by my
bedside
and the words seem to escape
the confines of the covers and bindings
making their way like vines
wrapping around the bed posts
leeching their way into my
thoughts
thoughts of you
thoughts of you and your room
how the light never crept in
unless you wanted it to
and when I was there my skin
shone like the sun itself, illuminated
the walls were dark
they seemed to be
closing in
but when I was there they glowed
orange and yellow

allowing projections of light
to fall upon them;
how your lips maintained a
downward curvature
until I was there to help you
smile
it is hard to fight in darkness
you won't know where your opponent
waits
and now that you've lost your light
I hope you don't lose your
way

poison oak

I found peace
in all the vines
that grew from your
veins,
I looked on in wonder
as you began to
grow;
but while you grew
I shriveled into a
pitiful existence
my dear
where there was seldom any
rain.

My leaves used to be evergreen
now they wilt and brown
and with my
tears I watered yours.

Vines that grow from your veins
no longer bring peace to my
heart
and I am no longer a girl who's
tears wet your soil and flood
your roots.

I've learned where giving ends.

You brought on my drought
of feelings
your vines are
poison oak
my dear,
I must leave now,
your vines are bound to choke
my dear,
and I have learned to
breath.

what they forgot to mention

what they forgot to mention was
that time apart means
darting eyes
sweaty hands
and
words that block the oxygen from ever reaching
your lungs
hurting is more than
broken hearts
cuts
and
bruises
emptiness,
that's hurting too

new beginnings

engraving her name on a new
trunk
one filled with treasures; gold
far from the nothing in the
old one— carved by him.

the humidity has made her dark
soil strands
lift up towards the sun; curls like
rays speeding in every direction.

nature's patterns engloving
her resistant body; strong—
her sorrow is alleviated by the sun
setting upon the previous chapter.

she draws a line in the sand; a border between her
and him.

he who found a place beneath
her solid branches by
displacing her.

shipwreck

marbled shades of blue
peak in frothy mountain tops;
sky and atmosphere blend seamlessly at the
horizon.
I guess how far I can see until my eyes succumb
to the illusion of the edge.
If I could set my worries free on a boat,
send them burning into the sunset,
I wonder if they'd sail freely
or stay anchored close to shore.
Lost in the stormy seas,
waiting for shipwreck,
I hope they'd sink gloriously to the depths;
unencumbered by their need to stay alive,
they'd drown among the fish and kelp and
decompose
before becoming a burden for someone else.
All that would be left is the boat that sailed them
to their fortunate demise.

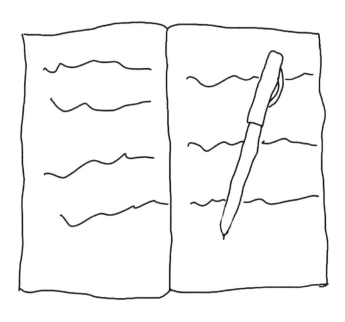

create

time traveling

the blinds shed strips of light
about the room
in these pockets of illumination
dust particles dance brilliantly
feet make contact with cold floors
and the quest for a cup of tea begins

warm water boils silently
chirping fills the air
birds awake with morning light
earl grey's aromatic scent fills
your nostrils as you begin to sip

closing your eyes
old buildings and rain seep from your memory
replaying vividly as though in front of you
a laugh you haven't heard in a while
blesses your ears with it's harmonious glow

and suddenly life is meant for time traveling
through remembrances and forgotten memories

how to cook the moon

If you start off sober you're wrong (doomed)
the lunar light will blind you by the time you put
it in the oven, so
enjoy the stars.

Slice a ravine into the dark side of it's cavernous
face,
let the liquid drip out.

Watch the juices trip over your fingernails
beating seconds into the cutting board.

Pierce the pip with the point of the knife and twist
manipulate it as best you can.
A cavalcade of waxing and waning memories.

Dice the plasma
ignore the sinews lacerating slowly
while solar systems preheat at four hundred fifty
degrees Celsius.

Break apart the spine until it shatters
into ore and slag
tossing it away.

hail avenue

Avenue fishing appeases eleven year old boys
jumping
backwards into already laced up shoes
Ivy revolves around pillars in Eden
Onions, bread, and soup remain in isolated attics
Floorboards share secrets with the tenants below

Bipolar on the topic of utopia he alleviates
his attention upward
He wonders if the eaves eavesdrop and pass the
message on
Oblivious, notorious, his
downtown Kiev in dreams, unperturbed

Two ovular ins and outs in seeing across you
and onto his
nostalgia inn

Hello avenue,
on par and waiting, ouroboros in nature
silence caves in and over approaching
already laced up gates, riddled with bullet holes

His pathos weighs him down
onus probandi and the burden of
wine whose novelty has not yet been tarnished by

smog, his
downtown Kiev in reality, disturbed

Eulogies being written for a city
ingesting it's own tail
all the while eleven
years have gone
and old boys are mourning

holy.

however hard it tries,
a breath will always be holy.
in urgent lungfuls of oxygen and powerful
exhalations
there is a sacredness.
we live in symbiosis with the trees
a heavenly relationship.

brown

miscarriage of language, a sudden thought
aborted
dwelling on the proposal of laughter, unsung in
space and time
java shooting through veins and stratum
to surface in punch and ebullience

ten
scarcely distant and moreover handsomely donned
in robes
morning brew served cold and unwanted:
the stillbirth of a eugeroic drug

stray feline
docile in its movements,   slips   by

the folly of words masquerading as magnum
opuses
affecting a fancied balance
written inquiries buried, soil bound.

clods fall into decay
woods lay dormant, awaiting the quiet breeze.

hat lovers bargain for misshapen brims
all the while
figs burgeon incarcerated by their own bandwidth.

lioness

lioness
from every angle.
not to say that you are not soft,
but you are stronger than you recognise.
earthly nourishment accounts for one percent of it
the other ninety nine — illustrious fire.
your fingertips will scorch whatever they touch
sending us all burning brightly into the world
with new purpose.
a voice quaking with splendour, eyes — an open
sea.

earthquake
from every angle.
not to say that you are not gentle,
but you can disrupt a broken world more than you
believe.
go on, disrupt.
we watch as you shake the universe
all with just your pinky finger.

sewing seeds

she stood at the back garden gate

wind disturbing her hair, like a tender hand
unearthing a secret

only to plant it in the soil again.

freckles littered the pale planes of her skin

and if you concentrated long enough you could
begin to make out

strangely abstract faces;

she was adorned in tiny works of art.

there were things you could tell about her by the
way she spoke.

it was like she was sewing seeds with each syllable,
each sound.

bound.

her spine is bound.

each vertebrae laced with string.

the core of a well used girl remains

though the pages fray and tear.

page 246 has a coffee stain in the bottom right
hand corner

right next to the wrist.

the story still flows from the lips,

written in a font that sounds lovely to the ear.

creases mark the habits of a well loved girl;

margins full of other people's thoughts.

she evolves, though bound, she is never finished.

Ingram Content Group UK Ltd.
Milton Keynes UK
UKHW052120130323
418475UK00011B/102

9 780368 443961